Out of this World

PLANET OF WINDS

by Sally Odgers

illustrated by Georgina Thomas

D1079534

SCHOLASTIC

THE ARKIES

This 2009 edition published in the United Kingdom by
Scholastic Ltd
Villiers House
Clarendon Avenue
Leamington Spa
Warwickshire
CV32 5PR

First published in 2007
by Macmillan Education Australia Pty Ltd.

Text by Sally Odgers
Illustrations by Georgina Thomas
Cover Design Allison Parry
Design by Matt Lin/Goblin Design
Managing Editor Nicola Robinson

Out of this World: Planet of Winds
ISBN 978 1407 10111 8

Printed by Tien Wah Press, Singapore

1 2 3 4 5 6 7 8 9   9 0 1 2 3 4 5 6 7 8

Contents

Characters

The Arkies

Singer

Gentle Singer can sense the mind of any living being, and communicate by thought alone. She understands many languages.

Lyam

Science whiz Lyam can tell the Arkies everything they need to know about alien plant and animal life – and then some.

Merlinna

Merlinna is always ready for a battle. She's an expert with weapons – including her naturally piercing screech.

Pace

Pace is a practical guy with a very practical skill – he can communicate with electronic equipment. He and Singer are special friends.

EarthNet

Tench and Farla are EarthNet agents who trail the *Ark3*. They want to capture the Arkies and return them to Earth.

Tench   **Farla**

THE ARKIES ARE TEENAGERS WHO ACT AS PATHFINDERS, SEEKING NEW, SETTLEMENT-READY (S-R) PLANETS. SOMETIMES, LIFE ABOARD THE ARKIE EXPLORATION SHIP ARK3 IS DANGEROUS AND EXCITING. SOMETIMES ... WELL ... IT ISN'T!

HOW LONG SINCE WE LAST LANDED ON A PLANET?

TOO LONG. THERE AREN'T MANY PLANETS IN THIS PART OF THE GALAXY.

AND ARKMA SAYS MOST OF THEM ARE UNSUITABLE FOR LANDING. THERE WAS THE ONE WHERE ALL THE PLANTS HAD THORNS.

AND THE ONE WHERE NO ONE COULD DRINK THE WATER.

SINGER, HAS THE ABILITY TO SENSE LIVING MINDS.

I'M SENSING SOMETHING. PACE, GET ARKMA TO CHECK FOR ANY PLANETS NEARBY.

PACE TRIES TO COMMUNICATE WITH THE MATCON, THE TOOL THAT CONVERTS MATTER FROM ONE STATE TO ANOTHER.

LITTLE BRO? LITTLE BRO, WAKE UP!

Ark3

PACE? IS ANYTHING WRONG?

I THINK THE MATCON HAS LOST ITS CHARGE. IT'S TOO LONG SINCE I'VE HAD IT IN THE WIND OR SUN.

SWING IT AROUND YOUR HEAD. THAT WORKED BEFORE.

WHEW! LUCKY WE WERE STRAPPED IN.

I THINK I SAW SOMETHING OUTSIDE!

WE APPEAR TO HAVE ARRIVED IN THE MIDDLE OF A CATEGORY 3 CYCLONE.

THAT SOUNDS BAD. CAN WE LAND?

THE WINDS ARE LESS TURBULENT LOWER DOWN. TOUCHDOWN NOW IMMINENT. 5, 4, 3, 2, 1 ...

IT LOOKS PRETTY WILD OUT THERE.

GOOD. JUST WHAT I NEED TO RECHARGE THE MATCON. IS IT SAFE, SINGER?

SINGER SENDS HER MIND OUTSIDE THE ARK3, "FEELING" FOR LIFE FORMS, "DIDGIES".

THERE ARE DIDGIES OUT THERE BUT THEY'RE NOT HOSTILE.

MAYBE THAT'S WHAT I SAW. ARE THEY INTELLIGENT?

THEY'RE HAPPY!

THAT'S WHAT I LIKE TO HEAR!

EVEN THOUGH IT DOES MEAN THE PLANET ISN'T S-R.

THE ARKIES STARE AS THE DIDGIES OF THE WINDY PLANET APPROACH.

THOSE BIG ONES LOOK LIKE GIANT KITES.

AREN'T THEY BEAUTIFUL?

YUP.

AND VERY BIG!

WHAT ARE THOSE FUZZY BEE-THINGS?

I DON'T KNOW, BUT I THINK THEY'RE GRABBING A FREE RIDE.

ER ... SINGER, THEY'RE GETTING CLOSER.

THEY'RE SO BEAUTIFUL.

LITTLE BRO. HOW'S THE RECHARGE? HURRY IT UP, HUH?

HEE-HEE-HEE.

HEE-HEE-HEE.

HELLO FUZZYBEES.

WOW!

THE DIDGIES CROWD AROUND THE ARKIES. EVEN THE FUZZYBEES ARE BIGGER THAN THEY ARE.

MERLINNA WORRIES THAT HER WEAPON, THE TANGLE-LINE, WILL BE NO USE HERE.

THE TANGLE-LINE WOULDN'T BE MUCH USE AGAINST THOSE BIG ONES

IT'S OK, YOU GUYS. THEY LIKE US.

LO UZZYEE.

AREN'T YOU A GREAT LITTLE FUZZY FELLOW.

HEE-HEE-HEE.

HEE-HEE-HEE.

THE ARKIES HAVE NEVER HAD SUCH A WELCOME FROM DIDGIES BEFORE.

- 16 -

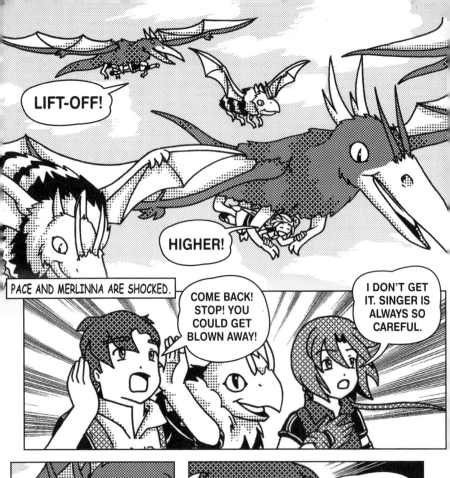

LIFT-OFF!

HIGHER!

PACE AND MERLINNA ARE SHOCKED.

COME BACK! STOP! YOU COULD GET BLOWN AWAY!

I DON'T GET IT. SINGER IS ALWAYS SO CAREFUL.

I OR EE OO ONE ...

WE'LL HAVE TO FOLLOW THEM, BUT WE'LL NEVER KEEP UP. THE WIND IS TOO STRONG.

WE WILL IF WE TRAVEL THE SAME WAY.

THE ARKIES SAIL OVER THE STRANGE PLANET, HANG-GLIDING FROM THE GIANT KITEWINGS.

GOOD. IT WON'T BE TOO FAR TO WALK BACK TO ARK3.

LOOKS LIKE WE'RE GOING DOWN.

IF WE CAN MAKE IT AGAINST THIS WIND.

PACE AND MERLINNA ARE COMING IN TO LAND.

ISN'T IT WONDERFUL?

MY KITEWING IS REALLY PLEASED. SHE SAYS I DID WELL.

ELL, ELL. UZZYEE.

HUH? THEY'RE TALKING TO US?

PACE DISCOVERS THAT LANDING IS NOT AS EASY AS IT LOOKS.

OH NO! I'M SLIPPING!

ARGH!

OOOF!

THE SECRET OF A GOOD LANDING IS NOT TO FALL.

GEN GEN, UZZYEE.

SHE MEANS YOU NEED TO TRY AGAIN.

I SEE.

UZZYEE???

THE KITEWINGS ARE NATURAL COMMUNICATORS, PACE. THEY PICK UP WORDS QUICKLY, BUT THEY CAN'T SOUND SOME LETTERS.

THAT'S BECAUSE THEY HAVE BEAKS INSTEAD OF LIPS.

UZZYEE?

THE ARKIES HAVE NEVER HAD SO MUCH FUN ...

UNTIL ...

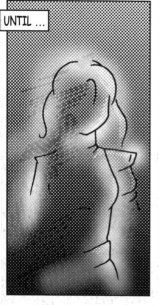

STOP THIS MADNESS IMMEDIATELY!

THE ARKIES ARE AMAZED TO SEE THEIR WORST ENEMY ON THE WINDY PLANET.

THAT'S FARLA FETTLEMAN!

INTERFERING AGAIN? CAN'T THESE EARTHNET GUYS EVER LEAVE US ALONE?

THE ARKIES LAND NOT FAR FROM THE EARTHNET AGENT.

WAIT. THIS IS WEIRD. LOOK AT HER HAIR.

IT ISN'T BLOWING.

I ALWAYS SAID SHE WAS REALLY A ROBOT.

WELL, FARLA? WHAT DO YOU WANT?

YOU ARE INTERFERING WITH THE INDIGENOUS INHABITANTS OF THIS PROHIBITED PLANET. YOU MUST LEAVE IMMEDIATELY.

WE KNOW WE CAN'T RECOMMEND THIS PLANET FOR SETTLEMENT, FARLA. WE'LL BE LEAVING SOON.

AGHH! UGH! GROSS!

THIS IS YOUR LAST WARNING. YOU MUST LEAVE IMMEDIATELY.

THE ARKIES SPRING FORWARD TO HELP THEIR ENEMY.

HOLD ON, FARLA!

SHE'S DONE FOR.

SUDDENLY ...

HUH? WHA—? BUT ...

WH – WHERE'D SHE GO?

I DON'T KNOW.

I *KNEW* THERE WAS SOMETHING ODD ABOUT HER.

HER HAIR WASN'T BLOWING, SO SHE WASN'T REALLY HERE. IT WAS A HOLOGRAM.

THE ARKIES LAUGH WITH RELIEF.

HAHAHA

SO, EARTHNET IS USING HOLOGRAMS NOW? I WONDER WHY?

THEY NEVER DID LIKE LANDING ON PLANETS.

IT'S FLYTIME!

LET'S GO!

LATER THAT DAY, ARKMA TRIES TO CONTACT PACE, BUT PACE DOESN'T HEAR.

PACE, WHERE ARE YOU? RESPOND.

REPORT TO ARKIE-PROGRAMME HEADQUARTERS. IT HAS BEEN SIX HOURS SINCE I HAD CONTACT WITH ARKIES PACE, MERLINNA, SINGER AND LYAM.

REQUEST URGENT ADVICE.

MAYBE I SHOULD GIVE THEM ONE MORE DAY ...

I'LL SEND THE REPORT TOMORROW ... SOON, ANYWAY.

MEANWHILE, THE ARKIES ARE HAVING FUN WITH THEIR NEW FRIENDS.

NO TROUBLE KEEPING THE MATCON CHARGED HERE!

JUST AS WELL I CAN USE IT TO MAKE FOOD AND SHELTER. ALTHOUGH ARKMA'S ALWAYS SAYING ... ARKMA!

YOU GUYS ... WHAT ABOUT ARKMA?

WHAT ABOUT HER?

WE OUGHT TO REPORT TO HER.

WHY? SHE KNOWS WHERE WE ARE. SHE CAN CALL IF SHE WANTS US.

I GUESS SO.

SINGER TOUCHES PACE'S ARM SO SHE CAN MINDTALK TO HIM.

Ark3

YOU SEEM WORRIED. IS EVERYTHING OK?

C'MON, SINGER, YOU KNOW I HATE MINDTALK.

OK, OK?

MINDTALK MAKES MY TEETH FEEL FUNNY.

WE CAN'T STAY HERE FOR EVER. WE REALLY SHOULDN'T HAVE STAYED SO LONG.

WE'RE NOT DOING ANY HARM.

PACE IS VERY READY TO BE CONVINCED.

I SUPPOSE NOT. THE KITEWINGS LOVE HAVING US HERE.

UV UV UZZYEES.

JUST A BIT LONGER.

chapter 4 : Trouble!

PACE IS TAKING A BREAK FROM FLYING WHEN ...

GEN, GEN, UZZYEE!

WHAT ARE YOU DOING? I NEED A REST.

SERIOUSLY I DO, YOU GUYS. I'M TIRED.

SLOW, UZZYBEE. NOT ELL.

HUH?

SINGER? COME HERE!

SINGER, STOP HER! SHE'S STRANGLING ME!

COMING, PACE.

WHAT IS IT? PACE, I THINK SHE WANTS YOU TO TAKE THAT OFF.

WHA—?

QUICKLY, PACE DOES AS THE KITEWING WANTS.

OK, OK, I'M DOING IT.

WHAT'S WRONG, KITEWING?

HEY! WHAT'S GOING ON?

I DON'T QUITE KNOW. SOMETHING SEEMS TO BE WORRYING HER.

ABOUT PACE? HE LOOKS THE SAME AS EVER TO ME.

KIND OF UGLY ...

I HEARD THAT.

UZZYEE NOT ELL.

HEY! HELP!

DID SOMEONE SAY SOMETHING?

UM. I THINK WE SHOULD GO BACK TO ARK3 NOW. THANKS FOR HAVING US.

WE REALLY HAD FUN, BUT WE DO HAVE TO GO. COME ON, YOU GUYS.

KERWALK!

THE ARKIES SET OFF FOR ARK3, BUT THEY DON'T GET FAR.

LET GO!

QUIT THAT! WE HAVE TO GO!

HEY! OUCH!

FLY! UZZYEES, FLY! FLY!

THEY'RE GOING TO FLY US BACK TO ARK3.

THAT'S ALL RIGHT THEN.

IS IT?

OK, ONE LAST FLIGHT, THEN.

ES, ES, UZZYEES.

ARKMA, HERE WE COME.

THE KITEWINGS ARE TAKING THE ARKIES FOR ONE LAST FLIGHT.

I'LL MISS THIS PLACE ... BUT I WON'T MISS THE WIND!

WAIT! THERE'S ARK3 BELOW!

TAKE US DOWN, PLEASE. DOWN THERE. DON'T YOU UNDERSTAND?

GEN, GEN, UZZYEES.

STOP!

THE ARKIES PROTEST, BUT THE KITEWINGS FLY ONWARDS.

STOP! TAKE US DOWN! AGHHHH!

SNAP!

OH NO!

NOW WHAT?

I DON'T KNOW.

LOOKS LIKE WE HAVE TO CLIMB DOWN AND WALK BACK.

USE THE MATCON TO MAKE US A LADDER, PACE.

UM ... I CAN'T. I DROPPED IT.

THE ARKIES ARE IN TROUBLE. WITHOUT THE MATCON, THEY CAN'T MAKE A LADDER, OR CONTACT ARKMA.

IT'S MY FAULT. I WAS SO SURE THE KITEWINGS WERE FRIENDS ...

SORRY, GUYS.

HEE HEE HEE.

POOR LITTLE FELLOW. HAVE THEY STRANDED YOU HERE AS WELL?

BRUTES. I'LL—

WAIT! WAIT A MINUTE. LOOK HERE.

LOOK AT WHAT? WE CAN'T HELP THIS LITTLE FELLOW. WE CAN'T EVEN HELP OURSELVES.

HE DOESN'T NEED HELP. DON'T YOU SEE? ... THE FUZZYBEES ARE JUVENILE KITEWINGS!

THEY'RE NOTHING LIKE KITEWINGS! THEY'RE FAT AND FUZZY AND STRIPED AND ...

CATERPILLARS AREN'T LIKE BUTTERFLIES, EITHER. HAVEN'T YOU NOTICED HOW THE BIGGER FLYING FUZZYBEES HARDLY HAVE ANY STRIPES?

LOOK. THE KITEWINGS TEACH THE FUZZYBEES TO FLY BY PARASAILING WITH THEM. THAT MAKES THEIR WINGS DEVELOP. THEY'VE BEEN DOING THE SAME WITH US. THEY THINK WE'RE BABY FUZZYBEES.

IS THAT BAD?

HEE HEE HEE.

MAYBE. IF THEY THINK WE HAVE TO STAY HERE UNTIL WE GROW WINGS.

WHICH WILL BE NEVER. OH! HOW COULD I HAVE GOT IT SO WRONG?

HEE HEE HEE.

YOU DIDN'T GET IT WRONG, SINGER. THEY ARE FRIENDLY. THEY'RE LOOKING AFTER US AS WELL AS THEY CAN.

THEY'LL HAVE GONE TO GET FOOD FOR THIS LITTLE GUY NOW ... AND FOR US. MERLINNA, GIVE ME YOUR TANGLE-LINE.

WHAT FOR?

WE'RE GOING TO USE IT TO ESCAPE.

GULP.

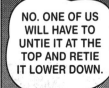

SURE. IS IT LONG ENOUGH?

NO. ONE OF US WILL HAVE TO UNTIE IT AT THE TOP AND RETIE IT LOWER DOWN.

chapter 5 : Wings

THE ARKIES USE MERLINNA'S TANGLE-LINE AS A SAFETY LINE WHILE THEY CLIMB DOWN THE TREE.

IT'S A LONG WAY DOWN. THE WIND MAKES IT ESPECIALLY DIFFICULT.

UGH!

PUFF!

THE ARKIES EVENTUALLY MAKE THE DIFFICULT DESCENT.

EVERYONE OK? LET'S GO. IT'S THIS WAY.

I HOPE.

DOES THIS WIND EVER STOP?

IT SEEMS A VERY LONG WALK.

EVENTUALLY ARK3 COMES INTO VIEW.

LOOK IT'S ARK3, HOW LUCKY IS THAT?

SOMETIMES THEY HAVE TO HIDE.

UGH-UGH ... HERE THEY COME AGAIN. HIDE!

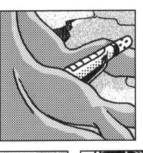

IS THAT ... ??

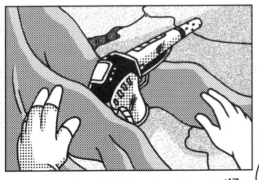

- 43 -

LOOK WHAT I FOUND!

AM I GLAD TO SEE YOU, LI'L BRO!

WE'RE GETTING CLOSER.

ARKMA? CAN YOU HEAR ME?

PACE? WHERE ARE YOU? I WAS JUST ABOUT TO SEND A REPORT TO SAY YOU WERE LOST!

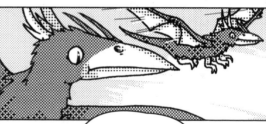

PACE IS STILL TRYING TO EXPLAIN WHEN MERLINNA SHOUTS AN ALARM.

NO, I DO NOT. I'VE ONLY ONE THING TO SAY TO YOU, PACE ...

YOU'RE GROUNDED!

LOOK OUT!

SO YOU SEE HOW IT WAS ...?

UZZYEES! UZZYEES! FLY! UV OO, UZZYEES!

- 44 -

LOGGING YOU IN, ARKIES.

BUT LYAM IS CAUGHT.

OUCH!

PULL!

WHAT DO YOU THINK WE'RE DOING?

UZZYEES!

MADE IT!

THANKS, YOU GUYS.

CLOSING HATCH!

UZZYEES!

ONCE THE ARKIES ARE SAFE, ARKMA DEMANDS A FULL STORY.

PACE FINISHES HIS REPORT.

SO THAT'S WHAT HAPPENED.

I SEE. SO THE DIDGIES ARE NOT HOSTILE BUT JUST DIDN'T UNDERSTAND HUMANS.

WE WERE FOOLED BY THE FACT THAT THE JUVENILE KITEWINGS LOOK SO UNLIKE THE ADULTS. IT WAS A SIMPLE ERROR.

UZZYEES!

NO HARM DONE. WE CAN GO NOW. OK?

NOT OKAY!

ARKMA HAS NEVER BEEN SO ANGRY WITH THE ARKIES BEFORE.

BUT ARKMA—

NO "BUTS"! YOU HAVE BEEN IRRESPONSIBLE, STUPID, FECKLESS AND CRUEL! HOW IS THAT "OK"?

CRUEL?

YES, DON'T YOU SEE? THE KITEWINGS ARE REALLY UNHAPPY AND IT'S OUR FAULT.

WE MADE A MISTAKE, AND WE HAVE TO FIX IT. I HAVE AN IDEA.

SINGER EXPLAINS HER PLAN AND THE ARKIES GET BUSY.